Sign Language
& Emotions

Bela Davis

Abdo Kids Junior
is an Imprint of Abdo Kids
abdobooks.com

Abdo
EVERYDAY SIGN LANGUAGE
Kids

abdobooks.com

Published by Abdo Kids, a division of ABDO, P.O. Box 398166, Minneapolis, Minnesota 55439.
Copyright © 2022 by Abdo Consulting Group, Inc. International copyrights reserved in all countries.
No part of this book may be reproduced in any form without written permission from the publisher.
Abdo Kids Junior™ is a trademark and logo of Abdo Kids.

Printed in the United States of America, North Mankato, Minnesota.

052021

092021

 THIS BOOK CONTAINS
RECYCLED MATERIALS

Photo Credits: Shutterstock

Production Contributors: Teddy Borth, Jennie Forsberg, Grace Hansen

Design Contributors: Candice Keimig, Pakou Moua

Library of Congress Control Number: 2020947662
Publisher's Cataloging-in-Publication Data

Names: Davis, Bela, author.

Title: Sign language & emotions / by Bela Davis

Description: Minneapolis, Minnesota : Abdo Kids, 2022 | Series: Everyday sign language | Includes online
     resources and index.

Identifiers: ISBN 9781098207007 (lib. bdg.) | ISBN 9781098207847 (ebook) | ISBN 9781098208264
     (Read-to-Me ebook)

Subjects: LCSH: American Sign Language--Juvenile literature. | Emotions--Juvenile literature. | Feelings--
     Juvenile literature. | Language and emotions--Juvenile literature. | Deaf--Means of communication--
     Juvenile literature. | Language acquisition--Juvenile literature.

Classification: DDC 419--dc23

Table of Contents

Signs and Emotions

ASL is a visual language. There is a sign for every feeling!

FEELINGS

1. Open one hand with palm facing body

2. Angle middle finger downward while keeping it straight

3. Brush middle finger a couple of times over heart

James had a great day.

He is happy.

HAPPY

1. Bring one hand to chest with a flat palm
2. All fingers should be touching with thumb out
3. Brush hand up toward heart a couple of times

7

Max had a bad day.

He is mad.

MAD

1. Make a grumpy face

2. Bring open hand up in front of face

3. Bend fingers toward face, making a claw

9

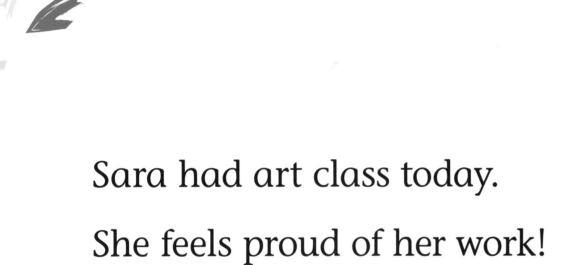

Sara had art class today.

She feels proud of her work!

PROUD

1. Make a fist with thumb pointing down
2. Touch thumb above belly button
3. Brush thumb upward toward chest

11

Dale is excited. It is

his birthday!

EXCITED

1. Hold both hands up near chest
2. Spread all fingers out
3. Angle middle fingers downward while keeping them straight
4. Move hands up and down

13

Rover is sad. He lost his bone.

SAD

1. Make a sad face
2. Bring open, upright hands above eyes with palms toward the face
3. Pull hands down toward the chest

15

Jess is reading a ghost story.

She is scared!

SCARED

1. Hold two fists in front of chest with palms facing body

2. Open both hands quickly with palms still facing body while making a scared face

17

Hue feels a little guilty. He ate a treat before dinner.

GUILTY

1. Make the "G" sign
2. Hold hand just above the heart and tap chest

19

Kay feels nervous. She has
never gone down the big
slide before!

NERVOUS

1. Make a nervous face
2. Put hands up in front of chest
3. Shake both hands back and forth

21

The ASL Alphabet!

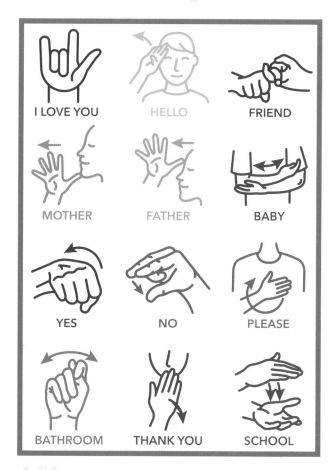

ASL

short for American Sign Language, a language used by many deaf people in North America.

guilty

affected by a feeling of having done something wrong.

Index

Abdo Kids
ONLINE
FREE! ONLINE MULTIMEDIA RESOURCES

Visit **abdokids.com** to access crafts, games, videos, and more!

Use Abdo Kids code

ESK7007

or scan this QR code!